BookRags Literature Study Guide

My Secret Garden: Women's Sexual Fantasies by Nancy Friday

Copyright Information

Table of Contents

Plot Summary

My Secret Garden: Women's Sexual Fantasies is a classic book by the writer Nancy Friday. When the book was first published in the seventies, it was highly controversial and condemned by leaders of the growing feminist movement. The book contains actual fantasies that real women have had, each one used to illustrate an element of the sexual fantasy. Nancy Friday intended the book to be a reassurance to all women that fantasy is normal and a healthy part of any sexual relationship. My Secret Garden is still controversial in some corners of the world, but its republication and high sales prove that fantasy touches the lives of all women, even those who are still afraid to admit to them.

The author, Nancy Friday, begins her book by describing a fantasy she once shared with a lover and his negative reaction to the idea that she was thinking of another man while engaged in sexual activity with him. This episode led Ms. Friday to wonder if having fantasies was abnormal and whether other women indulged in them. Ms. Friday began talking to her friends about fantasy and soon the idea for this book was born. Ms. Friday begins her book in this fashion in order to dispel the myth that not only do women not fantasize, but those who do are not normal. This myth, Ms. Friday came to realize in her research, was completely false. More women than those who will admit to it do fantasize.

Ms. Friday goes on to discuss the reasons why women fantasize. There are a number of reasons for a woman to fantasize. Some do it because their lover is inadequate, unable or unwilling to seek sexual satisfaction for their women. Others do it to enhance the experience of love making with their mate. Still others believe that fantasy can act as a sort of foreplay to the physical act. Some women fantasize in order to find the approval lacking in their intimate relationships while others do it because it is a safe way to explore sexual play in which they might not be willing to indulge in reality. Finally, some women fantasize to pass the day or to have a focus for masturbation, while others are simply unsatisfied in their reality.

Once Ms. Friday establishes the reasons why women fantasize, she begins to explore the themes that are present in almost every woman's fantasies. Ms. Friday presents sixteen themes that have been common to all the fantasies presented to her in her research for this book. These themes include being made love to by a stranger, or in front of an audience. Others include women who like to imagine being raped or physically beaten, while others like the idea of being completely dominated by a sexual partner. In that same vein, some themes include the idea of losing control or doing something that is completely forbidden, while others include the theme of transformation. Ms. Friday also suggests that some fantasies revolve around the idea of being motherly, caring for a lover, or even committing incest with various family members. Some of the more inventive themes include the use of animals or men outside of the woman's race, as well as young men or women. Finally, Ms. Friday includes the themes of fetishes and prostitution, but points out to her readers that only one woman spoke of a fetish and no women who responded to her request for fantasies mentioned the idea of being a prostitute, despite the fact that most experts believe prostitution is the most common theme of a woman's fantasies.

Next, Ms. Friday tackles the source of most women's fantasies. Ms. Friday explores the idea that a lot of women draw material for their fantasies from early childhood experiences, such as the first time a woman saw a naked man. Ms. Friday also insists that many women are more visual than experts give them credit for, becoming equally aroused at the sight of a naked man as a man might at the sight of a naked woman. Ms. Friday also explores the idea of guilt as a part of a woman's fantasy, suggesting that while a woman may feel guilty for the thoughts that come with her fantasy, these fantasies rarely include shame as many women have grown to believe they should. Ms. Friday also tackles the subject of a man's anxiety when made aware of his lover's fantasies and how this can add to the guilt a woman feels during or after indulging in fantasy.

Finally, Ms. Friday discusses the acceptance of fantasy. Ms. Friday interviewed and received letters from many women who were not only happy with their fantasies, but would often act them out either with a lover or on their own. Ms. Friday does not necessarily encourage a woman to act out her fantasies and she does not always advocate sharing them with one's lover. However, Ms. Friday feels that if a woman feels secure enough in her relationship and the safety of her fantasies, that no one should stop a woman from sharing her fantasies or acting them out. Ms. Friday ends her book with a short chapter on what she calls quickies, short fantasies that women shared with her and she in turn shares with her readers.

Chapter 1, Tell Me What You Are Thinking About, He Said Summary and Analysis

This book began as an exploration for the author to learn if her secret fantasies were normal and if other women had the same sort of fantasies as she does. The author was surprised by the number of responses she got from her requests for fantasies. The author took those responses and explored the reasons women fantasize and the types of fantasies women have.

Nancy Friday once had a lover who understood that humor was an important part of love making. When this lover once asked her what she was thinking during love making, Ms. Friday was honest and revealed in detail a fantasy she was having about being made love too during a football game. The lover did not find the fantasy entertaining and instead ended their activities and fled the home. Ms. Friday did not understand her lover's reaction and began to think there was something wrong with her desire to fantasize during love making. Ms. Friday never again told a lover about her fantasies until she met the man who would become her husband. When her husband accepted her fantasies and even encouraged them, Ms. Friday felt as though she had been released from the restraints her mother had placed on her as a child by refusing to acknowledge sex as a normal, healthy part of everyday life.

Soon after this release she got from her husband, Ms. Friday incorporated sexual fantasy in a fictional novel she was writing. Ms. Friday felt the fantasy enhanced the novel and gave a clear insight into the character. The publisher disagreed. The publisher felt that the fantasy made the character look like a sexual addict and that she should have focused on the lover rather than the fantasy. Ms. Friday felt her publisher's reaction pinpointed a distinct difference between men and women. Men share their fantasies openly, discussing them in the locker room, while women hide them, forced to feel ashamed of their sexual thoughts and feelings. Ms. Friday felt that women needed to discuss their fantasies and to be able to compare them in order to break out of the restraints placed on them by their mothers and society as a whole.

Soon after Friday's experience with the publisher, the sexua
began. Suddenly everyone was interested in what women th
Now women began to write about their own thoughts instead
what men thought women felt and thought about. The idea for
book was born and Ms. Friday began discussing the idea with h
friends and acquaintances. Ms. Friday was surprised at the reaction she
got. Men would become nervous while women would stop talking.
The consensus seemed to be that women did not have fantasies. In fact,
when men were around, it seemed no woman did. Ms. Friday stopped
bringing up the subject around men. However, when she got her
female friends alone, Ms. Friday was able to explore with them the idea
of fantasy. At first women would deny having fantasy, but when Ms.
Friday would describe a fantasy or two, the women would suddenly
recognize their own thoughts and feelings as fantasy. However, Ms.
Friday soon came to realize that her small group of friends and
acquaintances would not be enough to provide the research she truly
needed, so with the encouragement of her husband she began placing
ads in various publications seeking fantasies from women of all walks
of life. The response was overwhelming. Women were relieved to
finally have someone with whom to share their fantasies.

This chapter is a brief explanation of how the book came to be written.
Ms. Friday relates her personal experiences with a lover who was
shocked to learn that she thought about other men while making love to
him. Although Ms. Friday felt she was very open and liberated about
sex, she suddenly felt as though she was abnormal. Ms. Friday fell into
the cycle she had thought she had broken, the same inhibitions that she
saw and learned from her mother. However, when Ms. Friday met the
man who would become her husband and found in him support for her
fantasies, she again began to explore the her sexual fantasies by writing
about them in a fictional novel. Unfortunately, this book was rejected
by her publisher, causing Ms. Friday to reevaluate society's views on
women and sex. All of this led Ms. Friday to making the choice to
write this book and begin gathering information on sexual fantasies.

Ms. Friday has presented to the reader her perspective on sexual
fantasies and allowed the reader to see some of her own fantasies as
well as the reactions of the men in her life to these fantasies. This sets
the tone for the novel, allowing the reader to see that Ms. Friday comes
to this subject with her own opinions, removing the objective tone and
allowing the reader to see where the author is coming from when she

egan writing this book. Ms. Friday also tells the reader that her own opinion on female sexual fantasy changed while writing this book as a result of the fantasies she received from the many women who responded to both her requests for interviews and her ads requesting letters regarding fantasies. Finally, this first chapter explains the structure of the book and lets the reader know that all the fantasies included in the book are from real women who openly shared their fantasies with Ms. Friday with both promises of anonymity and relief at finally finding someone with whom they could share this often secret side of their sexual lives.

Chapter 2, Why Fantasize When You Have Me?
Summary and Analysis

Ms. Friday explores the reasons why women fantasize. The first reason Ms. Friday gives is frustration. Madge, the first woman from whom Ms. Friday received a fantasy, talks about a fantasy she has involving a strange man, his woman, a dog, and a child. Madge claims that she has this fantasy because her husband does not attempt to give her pleasure during their sexual activity. Dot, another married woman, claims that her husband stopped attempting to give her pleasure after their wedding. As a result, Dot often fantasizes about making love with a stranger. Insufficiency is another reason Ms. Friday explores, using the fantasy of Louella, a woman whose husband refuses to have sexual relations with her. Due to this fact, Louella has fantasies about her husband's minor child. Another woman, Irene, is married to a man who is highly intelligent and working toward a master's degree, and therefore has little time to indulge his wife's needs. Irene's fantasies focus on herself, and she imagines herself to be both a man and a woman and making love to herself. Annette is a young woman married to a man who travels frequently, leaving Annette alone with her fantasies to satisfy her personal needs. Finally, Maria has been married three years and uses fantasy to enhance her experiences with her husband, though she does not tell him because he is insecure about his own sexual attractiveness.

Another reason Ms. Friday believes women fantasize is to enhance their sexual experiences. Ms. Friday believes that a woman's mind is as important to her sexual satisfaction as her body; therefore, fantasy is an essential part of a woman's sexual experience. Patricia agrees with this assessment, admitting that she often imagines her lover is performing oral sex on her while they are in a public place. Patricia shares this fantasy with her lover and as a result the sexual experience is further enhanced for both parties. Suzanne is a young woman who likes to fantasize about having sexual relations with a man she never sees. Suzanne's husband is aware of these fantasies and uses them to encourage Suzanne's excitement during their love making.

Ms. Friday moves on to foreplay. While Ms. Friday does not advocate sharing one's fantasies, she does admit that in doing so it can sometimes make the love making more exciting for both partners. Bertha, for example, believes that remembering past love making episodes with her husband helps to make less exciting episodes better. Bellinda, a woman whom Ms. Friday became aware of through letters to a noted psychologist, did not fantasize until the doctor told her it was okay to imagine another man making love to her during foreplay. This permission allowed Bellinda to truly enjoy sex for the first time in her adult life.

Ms. Friday goes on to discuss how some women fantasize in order to seek approval they were not able to get in reality. Sally is a friend of the author's who is often attracted to older men. In her fantasies, Sally is talking on the phone with her mother while a man or several men are making love to her. In these fantasies, Sally's mother is often kinder to her than she is in reality. Vicki is an independent woman who often picks abusive men as her lovers. Vicki's fantasies often revolve around a doctor performing a vaginal examine on her, ending with a proclamation of superior health. Francesca, who has an ambivalent relationship with her mother, often fantasizes of being brought before a woman who is to judge her sexual abilities before she is sold to a Rajah. Often in these fantasies, Francesca's mother is also involved in the process, either sexually or as an instructor. Sondra has fantasies that she is being made love to by an octopus in a painting while Jesus observes.

Exploration is another reason women tend to fantasize. In these fantasies, women often fantasize about things that they would not normally do in reality. Karen fantasizes about a sexual encounter with a female friend while Abbie likes to make love to her husband when he is fully clothed so that she can pretend that he is a woman. Hilda, a happily married woman, often imagines having sexual intercourse with a man while riding a bull. Heather likes to imagine herself making love to another man in the same room in which her husband is making love to another woman, while Kitty likes to imagine group sex with multiple partners.

From exploration, Ms. Friday turns her attention to sexual initiative. Many women have been told since they were very young that a young woman does not initiate sex, she simply lies passively while her lover does as he pleases. With the sexual revolution, this opinion has changed not only in the outside world, but in the bedroom as well. Carol, for example, likes to fantasize that she and her husband are a demonstration couple for a class designed to teach young men about sex. Faye loves the idea of initiating her lover into the world of group sex.

Ms. Friday believes that with a new attitude toward sex, women are finding sex more exciting and therefore more insatiable than ever before. Clarissa, though she declares her love making with her husband is very satisfying, loves to imagine being made love to by the enormous organ of a fertility statue. Annabel imagines making love with many men at once, while Iris likes the idea of a man examining her sexual organs closely. Nora is unhappy with her husband's variety in bed; therefore, she tells herself different erotic stories every night, similar to the tales in the Arabian Nights.

Daydreams are another way in which women fantasize in an attempt to fulfill needs while also staving off boredom or frustration. Corinne bases her daydreams off a story a friend once told her of how he was painting his apartment in the nude with a female friend and they made love after engaging in a paint-splattering fight. Molly likes to daydream about a young man who makes love to his teacher while she lectures him on his poor classroom performance. Alicia imagines she is hypersensitive on all her surfaces while Lily likes to imagine sexual activity with an ex-boss or black men she sees on the train. Several other women daydream about spontaneous sexual encounters, stimulation with inanimate objects, and indulging in oral sex during a boring lecture.

Masturbation seems to go hand in hand with fantasy. Many women only fantasize while masturbating or have special fantasies reserved for this one purpose. Ms. Friday found it to be interesting that most women had their first fantasy about the same time they first began to masturbate and that they rarely have fantasies during masturbation that involve active sex. Patsy masturbates often and when she does she recalls the first lesbian experience she had. Several of the other women listed in this section of the book imagine sexual experiences with door-to-door salesmen or former lovers, while others imagine lying in the ocean or remember sessions of mutual masturbation with their current lovers.

Finally, Ms. Friday presents the issue of the lesbian. Lesbians tend to have fantasies that are different from straight women. Lesbians often imagine that they are their own sex and another. Marion likes to imagine herself a man raping a motorcycle guy who then becomes a woman during their encounter. Others like to recall childhood experimentation, such as episodes with the family dog or seeing a man urinating in the woods. In this section, Ms. Friday has also included some fantasies from modern lesbians, including one from Susan who often fantasizes about an encounter with a female bartender in a local bar.

This chapter explores the reasons why women fantasize. The reasons are not all as simple as sexual frustration or dissatisfaction, despite the opinions of the experts at the time the book was originally written. Many women fantasize to improve their sex lives with their lover, whether or not the lover is aware of the fantasy. Women also use fantasy to help them become more excited for the love making session that is about to take place, as it were a form of foreplay. Other women simply daydream about sex in order to add a little spice to their mundane routines.

Ms. Friday does not just rely on her own perspective in this chapter but draws her conclusions from the many letters and interviews she has conducted in researching this book. Included in this chapter are fantasies received from these letters and interviews. Some of the fantasies are simple, without the inclusion of intercourse. Others are elaborate, with precise detail that would impress even the best erotic fiction writer. These different fantasies give example to Ms. Friday's arguments, emphasizing the arguments with real stories in a way that makes Ms. Friday's arguments seem logical and obvious.

Chapter 3, The House of Fantasy Summary and Analysis

Ms. Friday divides fantasies into sixteen rooms in a house similar to a brothel in order to categorize each theme within fantasies. These rooms are designed to be friendly places for women to come in order to indulge in the fantasies of their choice in a safe, if metaphorical, atmosphere. The first room is anonymity. This room is a place where women, such as Linda, Pamela, and Marie like to go to fantasize about a faceless man who often takes them from behind. In Linda's fantasy, she is in a hair salon with a curtain pulled up across her lap. A man on the other side of the curtain is employed to provide the women with oral pleasure. The man is not supposed to receive pleasure from this job, but the man working on Linda does, much to his detriment because the boss punishes him severely for his arousal.

Room two is the audience. This room is a place where women go to imagine a large audience watching and judging them during sexual activity. Woman like Caroline, Elspeth, Mary Jo, Melanie, and Celeste are excited by the idea of an audience approving of their sexual performance and cheering them on. For example, Celeste likes to imagine that she and her husband are making love in Madison Square Garden in front of a massive audience of men waiting to have their turn with Celeste.

Room number three is the rape room. Many women like the idea of being forced into sexual activity, even though they would not want to be raped in reality. This room is about letting go of inhibitions in a way that the woman does not have to be ashamed of afterward. Julietta, Gail, Dinah, and Sadie all like to think about a man forcing them to do something against their will. Gail's fantasy is based in part on fact. Gail was nearly raped by a young man whom she is still acquainted. This young man attempted to force Gail into sexual intercourse one night after a party, but stopped when Gail began to cry. Gail often imagines what would have happened if he had not stopped.

Room number four is about pain and masochism. This room is about control for most women, such as Barbara, Edith, Rose Ann, and Amanda. Rose Ann imagines that her limbs are being stretched in opposite directions, spreading her wide open until she rips apart and her bones break. Also included along this theme is room number five, which is about domination. These women tend to enjoy feeling low and being subjected to humiliation. Nathalie, Poppy, Heather, and Ingrid all enjoy the feeling of being out of control, of being punished. Ingrid recalls a story she heard in which a husband punished his wife by tattooing every inch of her body. Although Ingrid would never get a tattoo, the idea excites her to the point where she began collecting pictures of tattoos.

Room number six, similar to the previous rooms, is the sexuality of terror. This room is more about intense fear than it is about domination or pain. In this room, women are excited by a loss of control. Joanna was raped in her home and uses the memory of the terror she felt during this attack as a sexual fantasy. Ann, on the other hand, allows her mind to fall into the infinite blackness of space during sex, falling through this darkness like a spaceship out of control. In this way, Ann is able to let go of control and enjoy the sexual act.

Room number seven is the thrill of the forbidden. This room is all about doing things that they have been taught is forbidden or immoral, such as having an affair. The women in this room fantasize of things such as making love with an acquaintance during a game of hide and seek, such as Emma's fantasy, or of her husband becoming aroused in public as Donna imagines.

Room number eight is the transformation room. In this room, women imagine themselves more beautiful and graceful than they are in reality. Some women imagine themselves the most beautiful woman or the most alluring when they fantasize rather than the reality of a few extra pounds, as with Monica who is a young, plain woman, or Betty who becomes another woman all together in her fantasies. Room number nine is the earth mother room. This room is filled with woman who are excited at the idea of their own fertility. Vivian fantasizes during sexual intercourse that she is being planted, as though she is the ground in which a new seed will grow.

Room number ten is about incest. This room is not necessarily filled with women who were abused as children, although a few of these women do admit to inappropriate behavior, but rather a room filled with women who are simply excited by the idea of sexual intercourse between people who are related. Bella is one of these women. Bella is a nurse who once had an affair with a man who would call her sister during intercourse. Dominique likes to imagine herself as a prostitute who is hired to teach a young man about sex while his father watches. Lola takes memories of brotherly instruction a step further and imagines making love with her brothers as well as their wives.

Room number eleven is the zoo. In this room women fantasize about sexual play with animals, especially dogs. These fantasies most likely stem from a young woman's memory of seeing a dog's erection or the sight of barnyard animals mating on the farm. Jo dreams about the neighbor's large dog while Rosie discovered the eagerness of a dog by accident and uses the memory in her fantasies. Room twelve is filled with big black men. This room comes about by societal theory on a black man's size and sexual promiscuity. Some women see this room as forbidden as well, a connection between the races that is scandalous and immoral. Lydia and Margie imagine making love to black men, but Raquel finds herself excited over the idea of seeing herself with a black woman.

Room thirteen is young men. This room is not as busy as someone might think. Younger women is a common theme with men, but most women seem to like their men older and more experienced. There are a few, however, who enjoy this room. Both Evelyn and Victoria like to imagine themselves punishing young men until they reach a climax. Room number fourteen is like room thirteen in that it is a fantasy quite common with men, but rare with women. Room fourteen is the fetish room. Of all the fantasies Ms. Friday collected for this book, only one was about a fetish. Faith is what is called a urologenic. Faith fantasizes about urine.

Room number fifteen is one of the busiest rooms in the house of fantasy. Room fifteen is other women. Almost all women fantasize about being with another woman even if they do not consider themselves bi-sexual or lesbian. Ms. Friday does not believe that these fantasies are indication of latent homosexual desires, but rather a desire to be with someone gentle, caring, a mother figure of sorts. Many women sent in fantasies of other women for Ms. Friday's research, including Sandra who imagines a masculine woman who is both rough and passionate, gentle and caring. Some of these women came to these fantasies because of an attraction to a woman in reality, such as Stella who developed an attraction to a new acquaintance. Others fantasize about the experienced woman, the motherly figure, such as Rebecca, who imagines having an affair with a friend of her parents.

The last room in the house is room number sixteen, prostitution. When Ms. Friday first began researching this book, many experts told her that all women fantasize about being a prostitute. It seems that the idea of being a prostitute is so far outside of what defines most women that it allows them to fantasize with all their inhibitions gone. Being a prostitute gives a good girl the right to be bad. However, when Ms. Friday began to collect fantasies, she quickly discovered that while the idea of prostitution was mentioned frequently, it was always consequential and not the overall theme of the fantasy. Therefore this room is empty.

The chapter classifies some of the major themes of fantasy. Ms. Friday explains that most fantasies follow the same themes, although each woman brings to the theme a unique set of details that sets that fantasy apart from another woman's fantasies. By saying this, Ms. Friday allows the reader to comprehend the different categories without placing restrictions on fantasy for the reader that might discourage further fantasy for the reader. Ms. Friday seeks to explain fantasy and to express the normality of it, and for that reason she has categorized it. However, Ms. Friday does not wish to take away the uniqueness of fantasy; therefore, she is quick to express her opinion that all fantasies are unique no matter the theme.

Ms. Friday uses the metaphor of a house, not unlike a brothel, to separate the different themes into sections or rooms within the house. This use of metaphor makes it easier for the reader to understand the sometimes subtle nature between the different themes. The rooms, too, make it seem as though women who have these fantasies have a common place they can go to share and be safe with their own fantasies.

The themes vary by mere degrees within this house, but each theme is important to the overall fantasy and therefore important enough to be discussed. Rape, domination, masochism, and terror may all seem to be the same thing, but there are subtle differences that make it important for each to have its own room. However, fetishes and prostitution are so unimportant to most women that they hardly seem necessary to mention. Ms. Friday mentions these rooms because experts assign them to women and Ms. Friday has set out to dispel some of the assumptions about women and fantasy by writing this book. By Friday showing that few women have fantasies within these themes, she seems to have achieved that point quiet effectively.

Chapter 4, Where Did a Nice Girl Like You Get an Idea Like That? Summary and Analysis

Ms. Friday sets out to explain where some women get the ideas for their fantasies with childhood. Ms. Friday explains that many women begin fantasizing as young children and that these fantasies are set off by many things including the first time a young girl sees a penis, such as Lindsay who stumbled across a man urinating in the woods when she was ten. Others begin fantasizing when the vibrations in the car awake sexual feelings, as it did for Sonia, or spankings lead to sexual excitement as they did for Mona.

Sounds also seem to affect women in different ways, especially the sounds of sex. Some women enjoy conversation during sex and will often recall those conversations during fantasy, like Meg and Holly. When it comes to visual stimuli, many experts believe that women are not physically aroused by the sight of a naked person, be it male or female, as opposed to the almost instantaneous arousal a man might experience at the sight of a naked woman. However, Ms. Friday knows from experience that this is not true. Ms. Friday confesses that she is a crotch watcher, someone who likes to check out men's trousers while going about her busy day. Many women who responded to Ms. Friday's ads admit to the same habit. In fact, Deana wonders what the difference is between a woman looking at a man's crotch and a man looking at a woman's breasts.

At the same time, many experts believe that women are not aroused by reading erotic material or looking at sexy pictures. Again, Ms. Friday discovered that this was incorrect. Several women admitted to her that they like reading sexy stories or looking at their husband's pornographic magazines. Miranda often has erotic dreams of Greek gods while Stephanie had some of her most exciting fantasies after reading a book about Roman orgies.

This chapter deals with the question of where women get their fantasies. Ms. Friday lists several places, beginning with images from childhood. Children are highly impressionable and even though they often do not understand what is happening to their bodies, they do know when something feels good. These impressions lead to the earliest fantasies which are often built upon as a woman matures and learns more about sex. However, these first fantasies often remain the most exciting ones and therefore many women build on them to create their adult fantasy worlds.

Experts believe that women are not as visual as men. Ms. Friday refutes this by presenting examples of women who enjoy walking through their towns looking at men and imagining what they look like with their clothes off. Not only this, but women also like to read other people's accounts of sexual conquest. Women are a lot like men in this arena. Women take their fantasies from things as mundane as a newscast, imagining the newscaster with his shirt off, or more. Ms. Friday even adds her own personal story to this chapter, confessing to a love of crotch watching. Ms. Friday again asserts her perspective in this chapter and allows the reader to know that she is just another woman, like her contributors, who has sexual fantasies.

Chapter 5, Guilt and Fantasy, or Why the Fig Leaf? Summary and Analysis

As Ms. Friday conducted research on this book, she ran into a large number of women who denied having sexual fantasies until presented with examples of other women's fantasies. This, Ms. Friday believes, stems from the guilt almost all women feel about their fantasies. Once again the mother comes into this, a woman who repressed her daughter's sexual urges and made her feel ashamed. Women grow to learn that it is okay to indulge in the pleasures of sex, but still are afraid to share this pleasure with others. There is still that sense that to want to enjoy the pleasures of sex is wrong; therefore, even when the fantasy remains inside a woman's mind, she still feels guilty for even thinking those thoughts.

Christiana is a happily married woman who has simple fantasies about alternative sexual positions but is so convinced it is wrong that she refuses to share her desire with her husband. Other women, such as Hope, imagine making love with another woman or with many men, but again feel that these thoughts are dirty and she should not even think them. Adding to a woman's guilt about her fantasies is her lover. Men are often threatened by the idea of a woman's fantasy, especially when he learns that his lover is thinking of other men while making love to him. Men cannot control a fantasy man; therefore, they feel threatened. Some men even deny the idea, convincing themselves that their women could not possibly fantasize because he is so proficient at his love making. To illustrate this point, a man wrote to Ms. Friday and claimed that his wife never fantasized because he was such a good lover. This man even signed his wife's name to the letter.

This chapter discusses the guilt many women feel when they fantasize. Women have for so long been told they are the weaker sex, that they should be passive in bed, that they feel guilty when their minds are filled with ideas that do not fit into that ordered, puritan idea of sex. Ms. Friday provides several examples of this guilt, expressing how many women wrote to her and begged for anonymity in fear that their lovers or family might recognize their names. Guilt is one of the reasons Ms. Friday wrote this book, it was a motivation to end this guilt that helped create this project.

Ms. Friday also discusses a man's role in his woman's guilt, exploring the theme of sexual equality. Many men feel the need to be controlling in the bedroom. These men do not like the idea of his woman thinking about another man while making love. A man cannot control this aspect of his woman; therefore, he denies it is happening or becomes angry or insecure. This stops many women from fully embracing their own fantasies, leading to a deeper sense of repression. It is also this attitude on the part of the man that might stop a woman from acting out her fantasies in reality.

Chapter 6, Fantasy Accepted Summary and Analysis

Some women feel no guilt within their fantasies. These women often act out their fantasies in reality, sharing them with their lovers and embracing them without fear or shame. Some of these women who wrote to the author expressed their enthusiasm for their fantasies by announcing a need to satisfy their sexual excitement while simply writing the fantasy down on paper. Others express disbelief that any woman would deny having fantasies. Gloria believes her fantasy to be so perfect that a book such as this one cannot be published without its inclusion, while Hannah is so comfortable with her fantasies that she keeps photos of her fantasy men on her mirror. Sophie acts out her fantasies with her roommates, making her fantasy her whole world.

Some women are so accepting of their fantasies that, like Sophie, they sometimes become confused between what is fantasy and what is reality. Paula is one of these. Paula describes her fantasies to the author, describing sexual encounters with other women and group sex that includes her lover. As Paula describes this situations, the author becomes confused as to what has really happened and what remains a fantasy in Paula's mind.

The author touches on the idea of acting out one's fantasies. Ms. Friday does not advocate acting out fantasies that might be physically dangerous or harmful to a relationship. However, Ms. Friday believes that if a woman wants to act out her fantasy, then she should feel free to do so. Some women, such as Sylvia, have acted out their fantasy only to find themselves disappointed in the reality. Others, like Babs, are reluctant to act out their fantasies because of the impact it could have on their lovers or spouses. Still others, however, act out their fantasies with the full support of their spouses, and sometimes with the participation of their spouses. Jacqueline told her husband, quite by accident, about her fantasies of being with other men. Jacqueline's husband enjoyed the thought so much that he encouraged his wife to act out her fantasy. Ms. Friday even got a letter from a man relating how his wife's fantasies helped improve their sex life over the more than twenty years they had been married.

This chapter deals with the acceptance of sexual fantasies. While many women feel guilt over their fantasies, many others believe fantasy is a necessary part of their everyday lives. This chapter describes the confidence that many women have in their fantasies and the excitement that confidence brings to their lives.

At the same time, this chapter discusses the pros and cons of acting out and sharing fantasies. Some marriages are enriched by sharing fantasies, but others are damaged by it. The author expresses caution when acting out some fantasies, but encourages women to do what feels right for them. The overall theme of this book is that all women fantasize and that it is okay to fantasize. Therefore, it should be okay for women to accept this normal, healthy side of themselves and to embrace it in any way they feel fit.

Chapter 7, Quickies Summary and Analysis

This chapter simply lists a few short fantasies that women sent in to Ms. Friday that were not long enough to categorize or to garner anything of real significance. These tidbits are as similar as they are diverse, common to many of the themes discussed in chapter three, but so short that they do not offer insight into the minds of the women who wrote them. These are simply quick thoughts written by women who were fascinated by the idea of sharing their fantasies.

Important People

Madge

Madge is a woman who has been married to the same man for many years - a man who does not take an interest in his wife's wants and needs in bed. Madge's husband only makes love to her once every five to six weeks and these sessions are more for his sexual satisfaction than for hers. To compensate for her husband's lack of interest, Madge fantasizes during their sexual encounters. Madge imagines that she visits a home where there is a couple and a young child as well as their dog. The man forces Madge to participate in sexual acts with himself, the woman, and the dog while the young child watches. These fantasies help Madge achieve sexual satisfaction despite her husband's inattentiveness to her needs.

Patricia

Patricia is an American living in Rome with her lover while she is separated from her husband. Patricia and her husband have an understanding that they are both curious about other people and have agreed to separate only long enough for them both to satisfy their curiosity. Patricia likes to fantasize about a man performing oral sex on her while she is sitting in a formal location, such as an expensive restaurant. Patricia loves the idea of carrying on a normal conversation while her sexual excitement grows. Patricia always imagines that something exciting will happen just as she reaches her climax, such as the lights going out or an alarm sounding, to mask the sounds of her pleasure. Patricia likes to share this fantasy with her lover, though she has no plans of ever acting it out in reality.

Vicki

Vicki is a thirty-something single woman who works as an art historian. Vicki is often attracted to men who abuse her, both mentally and physically. Vicki denied having sexual fantasies until the author approached her about the subject of this book. Vicki has begun fantasizing and most of her fantasies are about doctors. While Vicki is engaged in sexual activity with her lover, she imagines a doctor is examining her, complete with a medical mask and gloves. The closer the doctor gets to make a diagnoses, the more excited Vicki gets, until the doctor announces that she is in perfect health. Vicki tells the author that her sex life has greatly improved since she began having these fantasies.

Patsy

Patsy is twenty-nine years old, married, but has not children. Patsy has fantasies about other women despite insisting that she has a good marriage and is not a lesbian. Patsy once had a sexual experience with a woman in a sauna, a friend who was bisexual. This friend introduced Patsy to the joys of making love with a woman. Since this experience, Patsy has used the memory to enhance her sexual relationship with her husband. Patsy's husband does not know about this encounter with her friend or that she uses the experience to increase her pleasure when with him. Patsy has no intention of telling him.

Kate

Kate is a lesbian who has a committed relationship with another woman. Kate married a man with the encouragement of her lover because it causes excitement between them when they discuss Kate's sexual relationship with her husband. Kate's lover often encourages her to tell her in detail the things that happen between husband and wife, using these experiences to become excited and to enhance their own love making. Kate's lover also encourages her to have other sexual experiences, such as making love in front of a mirror in order to watch her own body, and taking other lovers. Kate often draws on these varied experiences for her own fantasies.

Caroline

Caroline is a young actress. Caroline was in a play that included a scene in which she was to simulate making love to a man. The scene was intensely realistic. From the first time Caroline did the play, she began to imagine what it would be like to really make love to a man in front of an audience. Now, whenever Caroline is with her lover, she often imagines an audience watching her every move and reacting to each second of action. Caroline even imagines her lover is the actor with whom she enacts the scene on stage. Caroline dislikes the actor, but imagining his face above her during love making with her lover also serves to enhance the excitement.

Poppy

Poppy is a middle-aged, Catholic woman who has been married twice. Poppy draws on the memory of an affair she recently had to create fantasies while making love to her husband. These fantasies often include not just the lover, but his wife, and certain members of his family. Poppy imagines being forced to perform sexual favors on all these people as well as allowing them to perform certain sex acts on her. Poppy's fantasies also include a certain amount of degradation, both from the family members against her as well as degradation she commits against the person of her choice. Poppy often ends her fantasy by whipping the person of her choice.

Marina

Marina moves around a lot and has most recently settled down in Boston. Marina enjoys the company of older, refined men. Marina is independently wealthy, but has somehow managed to remain innocent despite her wealth and her nomadic lifestyle. Marina learned about sex from a girlfriend when she was only ten. The girl's father was a gynecologist, so she clearly knew all there was to know about sex. Marina was disbelieving when her girlfriend told her what sex was all about, but with experimentation began to understand the joys of sex.

Margie

Margie is a former model who now lives in the suburbs with her husband and is filled with boredom. Margie has fantasies about making love to a black man. Margie often lies in a bathtub full of perfumed water and allows the water to flow over her erotic zones while she imagines making love to movie stars like Harry Belafonte. Often these fantasies include the idea of Margie's lover voiding his bladder over her body. Margie imagines this fantasy might stem from a time when a ex-boyfriend voided his bladder on her while they were spending the day at the beach.

Evie

Evie is a divorced mother of two. Evie likes to remember things men said to her while making love. Evie becomes excited just by the memory of these words, suggesting that women are more interested in the sounds of lovemaking than experts might believe. Evie also mentions that she asked many of her friends about their fantasies, but many do not recall their fantasies, or at least say they do not when asked. Evie believes this is because women are not talkers, they simply like their men to talk.

Sophie

Sophie is only eighteen, but has been sexually active for many years.

Sophie once had a fight with her parents over her sexual activity and ended up leaving home over it. Sophie lives in Chicago with two men who are dramatically different from one another. The one man is strong, good-looking, but often rough and angry. The other is more studious, quiet, and introverted. Sophie is having an affair with both men. Sophie and both men often share a bed together. Sophie imagines herself to be in love with both men. When the tougher man hurts Sophie, the more studious man often makes excuses for him and encourages her not to hate him. Sophie believes the weaker of the two men is also in love with the other man.

Paula

Paula is a Haitian who is a good friend of the writer's. Paula spoke about fantasies in an interview with the writer. Paula talks about how she likes to imagine other people in bed with herself and her lover. Paula not only likes the idea of sharing her lover with another woman, but also likes the idea of watching her lover make love with another man. Paula also likes to seduce women that she believes her lover is attracted to so that if he should act on his attraction, Paula is not as jealous because she seduced the woman first. Often Paula acts out her fantasies, inviting other people into her bedroom with herself and her lover. Paula's lover is aware of her fantasies and encourages them, but refuses to make love to another man.

Objects/Places

Interviews

The author conducted numerous interviews with her female acquaintances in order to ask about their fantasies. Many of these interviews are included in the book.

Letters

Many of the fantasies the author includes in her book were received through letters written in response to her ads and articles in various publications.

Ads

The author placed numerous ads in many publications asking for women to write to her about their fantasies. A large number of women responded and many of them are included in this book.

House of Fantasy

The house of fantasy is a metaphorical house that the author describes in order to categorize women's most common fantasies.

Vibrator

Some of the female contributors of the book mention using a vibrator during sexual intercourse or masturbation in order to add to the physical stimulation.

Electric Toothbrush

A few of the lesbians who contributed to the book mentioned the use of electric toothbrushes as sexual tools that would enhance their lovemaking.

Water

Some women who contributed their fantasies to this book mention water as a tool in sexual stimulation.

Clothing

Clothing, or the lack thereof, is an important element to many women's fantasies. Some women enjoy dressing up for their lovers while others are excited by going out in public without undergarments.

Erotica

Some of the women who contributed to this book mention that reading erotica helps to supply material for their fantasies.

Mirrors

Mirrors are an important element to some women's fantasies. Some women enjoy seeing themselves during arousal and intercourse.

Television and Movies

Television and movies provide some women with material for their fantasies. Some of these women fantasize about the actors in the shows or movies while others imagine the television actors as an audience to their sexual play.

Playboy

Playboy is a magazine that features naked pictures of women as well as articles of interest to men. Some of the women who sent in their fantasies mention this magazine either as a personal turn on or in wishing that a similar magazine would be published for women.

Themes

Sexual Guilt

A large number of the letters written to the author of this book include phrases such as, please do not publish my name, or I bet you have never heard anything like this before. A large number of women seem to believe that their fantasies are not normal or that by having fantasies the women themselves are not normal. This sense of oddity causes many women to feel guilty for having fantasies. Not only that, but the content of many women's fantasies cause them guilt. Women who were raised to believe it was improper to ask for what they wanted in bed or to even touch their own bodies find it difficult to reconcile that advice with the thoughts and feelings coursing through their healthy bodies. All of these things combine to make women feel guilty for experiencing the effects of a normal sex life.

Another source of guilt for some women is the fact that they fantasize during sex with their lovers or husbands. Many women are afraid to tell their lovers about these fantasies because they are afraid that the man will be offended or turned off if they knew their women were thinking of other men during sex. Some women have tried to tell their lovers about these fantasies only to be rebuffed or to cause their men to fall into a depression due to feelings of inadequacy or shame. As a result, many women chose not to share their fantasies with their lovers in order to protect their feelings and sense of self worth. It is because of all these factors that guilt is a major theme of this book.

Sexual Equalitty

The author of this book begins her introduction by discussing with the reader how she thought this book would be embraced by the growing women's movement that was taking place at the time the book was published. The author truly believed that by sharing with the world the fantasies many women have, she was opening a door on another secret that kept women apart from men. However, the book was not received well by the women's liberation movement. In fact, the author was said to not be a feminist when this book was published. This shocked the author as she believed that she should have been embraced by this community for proving that women are sexually equal with men in every facet of life.

Sexual equality between men and women is a movement that has been a source of much debate for many people since the time this book was written. Many people once believed and may still believe that women do not have the same erotic fantasies as men, nor are they aroused by the same things. Part of what the author of this book has set out to do is to disprove these beliefs. The author believes that women are equal to men in that they experience the same degree of arousal from visual stimulation as men. The author also hopes to point out that women fantasize as much as men, and in some cases, may fantasize more than men. It is apparent to the author that women have more reason to seek out additional stimulation and therefore it is more logical for a woman to fantasize than it might be for a man. In this sense, the author seeks to prove that men and women are fairly equal when it comes to sexual fantasy, making sexual equality a theme of the book.

Sexual Normality

Many women included in this book wonder if what they fantasize about his normal. Some women have fantasies that are so far outside the realm of what they might consider participating in in reality that they question their own mental health when it comes to sexual fantasies. Many women imagine having sex with animals or other women, causing them to wonder if there is something abnormal in their mental processes. Other women fantasize about rape and domination, things they would never want to have happen in real life. Still others imagine how wonderful it would feel to be spanked and tortured, but again would never want these things to take place in real life. These women are left asking if what they fantasize is normal or if it is a hint that they might need some sort of psychiatric health.

The author of this book set out to learn how many women have fantasies like the ones that she has herself. The author at first believed that fantasies were unique to a few individual women and not a common occurrence. The author herself was surprised to learn just how many women in the world have fantasies on a daily basis. Rather than prove herself unique, the author was able to prove that having fantasies was the norm. Not only this, but with the wealth of information the author received from women from all walks of life, she learned that fantasies could be simple and almost mundane to wild and exotic. Fantasies of lesbian experiences, rape, domination, and even bestiality were not odd or symptoms of mental disease, but completely common. The author proves through her research for this book that fantasy is normal, making sexual normality a theme of the book.

Style

Perspective

The author, Nancy Friday, is a woman who has had sexual fantasies most of her life. Ms. Friday recalls some of her fantasies in the introduction to this book, remarking on how a lover once became outraged when she told him of a fantasy she had while they were making love. This led Ms. Friday to become curious about other women's fantasies and whether there was something strange or abnormal about her own. Ms. Friday began telling some of her friends that she intended to write a book about sexual fantasies and quickly discovered that the very idea caused a great deal of excitement in her normally quiet and reserved friends. Conversations began about the most intimate details of these women's lives, beginning for Ms. Friday a path of discovery that not only led to this book, but to a career in the study of sexuality.

Ms. Friday's perspective is that of a woman who has had sexual fantasies. Due to the fact that this book is about the sexual fantasies that all women have, why they have them, and where they come from, Ms. Friday is highly qualified to write this book due to her own experiences. Ms. Friday is just like many of the women whom she writes about in this book. Ms. Friday has not only had sexual fantasies, but she has had the experience of both being shunned and accepted for these fantasies. Ms. Friday comes to the book with the same perspective of many of the women who share their experiences within its pages, making her an expert on the subject and a far better author for the subject than a man or clinical observer might be.

Tone

The tone of the book is subjective. The author discusses within the pages of this book fantasies that women who have written to her or spoken with her have shared. These fantasies are organized according to the subject of the chapter, such as why women fantasize and where their fantasies come from. The author cannot be objective about her subject because she has experienced many of the same things her readers have and therefore cannot look at the subject with any distance, as would be required for an objective point of view.

The tone of this book is intended to draw the reader in, to allow the women who read this book to feel as though they are not alone in their sexual thoughts and are not abnormal for having some fantasies that might be deemed unnatural or dirty by someone who does not understand or embrace sexual freedom. The tone is also meant to help men who read the book understand more about the way their lovers' minds work and how to understand their sexual fantasies in such a way as to be supportive rather than repressive. The tone of this book works for its intended audience because it is subjective rather than a clinical analysis of something that is far from clinical.

Structure

The book is divided into seven chapters. Each chapter tackles a different aspect of sexual fantasy. The chapters cover things such as the reason why women have fantasies, where the fantasies come from, and the different themes fantasies encompass. Within each chapter the author has supplied examples for each category she covers that consist of letters or excerpts from interviews that describe sexual fantasies or the thoughts behind them. Some of these examples include fantasies in erotic detail, showing the reader exactly what is going through a woman's mind as she fantasizes.

The book's structure works for the reader because it does provide so many examples of fantasies. These examples help the reader fully understand the point the author is trying to make in the preceding introduction. When the author talks about the different themes that fantasies can be divided into, the reader finds it helpful to read the examples because some of these themes are closely related to one another. The reader might also find it helpful to read these fantasies in order to find something of her own fantasy in them. This recognition allows the reader to understand that her own fantasies are normal and there is nothing shameful about doing something millions of women around the world are doing as well.

Quotes

"One of the things I had always admired in my lover was the fact that he was one of the few men who understood that there could be humor and playfulness in bed. But he did not think my football fantasy was either humorous or playful. As I said, he just left." Chap.1 p. 3

"Most people think women's sexual fantasies fill a need, a vacancy; that they are taking the place of The Real Thing, and as such arise not in moments of sexual plenty, but when something is missing." Chap. 2, p. 15

"If you like, you can read almost any female sexual fantasy as a cry of frustration. We are all prepared to think of women, any woman, as potentially frustrated simply because it is our historic sexual role. Traditionally, we are the frustrated sex--less experienced, less mobile, and less accepted sexually." Chap. 2, p. 27

"Many artists have painted the female nude, but each picture speaks to different audiences and different emotions, and in different ways. The theme is classic, or, if you like, 'stock'; the details are subjective, personal, and make the difference." Chap. 3, p. 124

"Rape does for a woman's sexual fantasy what the first martini does for her in reality: both relieve her of responsibility and guilt." Chap. 3, p. 146

"Whatever their reasons for wanting it, the domination fantasists long to feel low. They relish being debased and reduced by whatever means to a state of abject humiliation. How they get down there does not matter." Chap. 3, p. 167

"While I intend this book to be an introduction to the idea that female sexual fantasies exist and can be talked about, I do not pretend that my research can in any way be called complete." Chap. 3, p. 233

"To try to convey the emotion, meaning, and experience of sexual fantasy through euphemism would be like giving a thirsty man a piece of paper with the word 'water' written on it. It's either the real thing, or nothing." Chap. 4, p. 269

"I know popular theory has it that women are not as sexually aroused by what they see and read as men. Men are supposed to have this trigger response to the sight of a breast or a bottom; whole segments of our economy depend on it." Chap. 4, p. 299

"A woman's fantasy brings up in him the spectre of the unconquerable rival, with magical abilities and unimaginable proportions, and, above all, a rival over whom he has no control. Some men don't react with anger or panic, but with simple denial." Chap. 5, p. 340

"But accepting your fantasies can mean just that, and end right there; there's nothing that says you've only gone halfway if you don't act them out. Fantasy has no Hoyle's Book of Rules." Chap. 6, p. 375

"...I just think how much I love him when we make love. But every once in a while, I play the pussycat and he the affectionate owner..." Chap. 7, p. 415

Topics for Discussion

Discuss fantasy. What constitutes a fantasy? Are all fantasies alike? Does a fantasy necessarily have to include a sexual element to make it a fantasy? Do all people fantasize about the same things? Why or why not?

Discuss some of the reasons women fantasize. How does fantasy help a woman? Can fantasy enhance a relationship? Can fantasy make a relationship less fulfilling? Are all fantasies born out of dissatisfaction? Why or why not? List some of the reasons the author gives for women's fantasies. What is similar about these reasons? Are all these reasons negative? Give some examples of positive reasons to fantasize.

Discuss the themes that often come up in fantasy. How many different themes does the author list? Are all these themes unique? What is similar about some of these themes? What is different? Are there any other themes you can think of that the author has not mentioned? How have some of these themes changed in the thirty years since the book was written? Why?

Discuss the sources of fantasies. What about a woman's childhood could cause material for fantasies? Describe how something innocent can become material for a woman's fantasies. Why do some things have such a strong, sexual influence on a woman when seen as a child?

Discuss visual stimulation. Can a woman become aroused by the sight of another person? Why do some experts believe this is not true? Is it wrong for a woman to look at a man the way a man looks at a woman? Why or why not? Can a woman become aroused by erotic literature? Why or why not?

Discuss a man's reaction to his lover's fantasies. Why are some men threatened by fantasy? Should a woman tell her lover when she is fantasizing and what it is about? Discuss some of the dangers of sharing a fantasy with a lover. Discuss some of the benefits of sharing fantasies with a lover. Based on the stories in the book, do you think it is beneficial to a relationship to share fantasies? Why or why not?

Should women be encouraged to act out their fantasies? What are some of the pros and cons of acting out fantasies? What types of fantasies should not be acted out? What types should be acted out? Who should make the ultimate decision when it comes to acting out a fantasy? What should a lovers role be in acting out his lover's fantasy?

Made in the USA
Las Vegas, NV
11 January 2024

84215035R10028